LEAR ANANCI

ACTOR: BRIAN HONORE AS KING LEAR IN THE
UNIVERSITY OF THE WEST INDIES' PRODUCTION
OF DAVLIN THOMAS' **'LEAR ANANCI'**.

CHARACTERS

Ananci/Fool

King Lear

Cordelia (Lear's daughter)

Regan (Lear's daughter)

Goneril (Lear's daughter)

Gloucester (The Earl)

Edgar (Gloucester's son)

Edmund (Gloucester's son)

The Television

The Announcer

Professor Reinhart

Guard 1

Guard 2

DAVLIN THOMAS'
LEAR
ANANCI

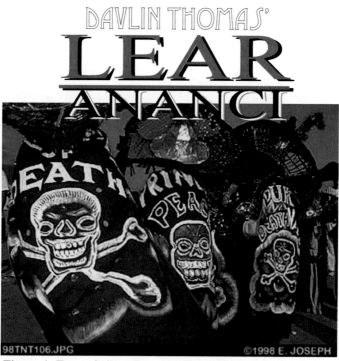

98TNT106.JPG   ©1998 E. JOSEPH

Figure 1: Fancy Sailors Dancing(Trinidad Carnival)

(A television set suddenly produces the only light in the room)

Announcer - Good evening ladies and gentlemen,

This is a live update from the Capital city of Port of Spain

I'm afraid the situation here today is very much the same as before.

The Red House has been bombed.
And as most viewers already know,
Parliament was in session when the bombing occurred.

The explosion engulfed both members of Government and the   opposition...the situation has had some rather interesting side effects.

Earlier today, at least 10 hours after the initial explosion

Members of Parliament were seen on the grounds of the Queens Park   Savannah. Eye witnesses report that Parliamentarians seem to drift back and forth from reality like ghosts enacting some sort of live play.

what is significant though is that neither of them respond to any contact   whatsoever from anyone who has attempted this.

With us this evening is Professor Max Reinhart of the University of the   West Indies who will attempt to offer some explanation for the phenomenon. Professor Reinhart..

Professor - Thank you Sylvia.

The key to any possibility of explanation for this Phenomenon lies with the   fact that no members of parliament seem to be able to recognize or   acknowledge any components of our reality.

Announcer - so you're saying that..

Professor - let me finish, please. All those persons who have.. appeared at the Queens   Park Savannah as part of the Ghostly play that is happening over and over at sites throughout Trinidad and now we have heard, throughout the Caribbean, are Members of The Trinidad Parliament, except for Ananci who we think is the embodiment of the Caribbean people and I will tell you why.

   We at the University believe (he turns to diagram) that when the Bomb   destroyed Parliament during the debate of the Equal opportunities Bill, the intensity of the arguments being presented and of course the intensity of   the bomb itself caused a fusion of time, physical space and consciousness that has endured beyond the persons and the event itself.

Announcer - Professor Reinhart, could you please simplify this for us and the viewing   audience?

Professor - Well, the truth is that the bomb was so powerful that it blew Parliment into   an entirely different reality...its as simple as that.

Announcer - I understand the concept, but why does this look so much like a play?

Professor - isn't that exactly what a play is, an entirely new reality that is derived from the   current one and is therefore reflective of that reality even in the ideological and philosophical challenges that the 'play' world presents for the parent reality.

Announcer - I don't understand.

Professor - you should go to the theatre more often...

(Pause)

Announcer - We have had enough experience with the phenomenon to know that the   entire spectacle takes a total of about two hours, then all players disappear to   reappear elsewhere within the Caribbean. Includiing this Ananci character who seems to be presenting th, the, the, thing. Could you tell us more of this Creature.

Professor - Well, I don't know, except to say that like the mythical story teller whose   name he carries, this Ananci seems to have woven our Parliament into a play of reality altering proportions.

Announcer - any idea when this may end?

Professor - we don't know.

Announcer - any idea what we should do in the interim?

Professor - well, sit back and enjoy the play, you may learn something.

Announcer - thank you Professor.
Ladies & Gentlemen
If the phenomenon occurs in your area, "sit back & enjoy"

a simple answer to a very complex problem.

This is Sylvia Gall from TTT news saying, goodnight.. and God bless.
(The television switches off)

Voice - Ananci Oyeeee!!!!

(A dance begins and ends, it tells of the spider who weaves plot, story and web and that the is the audience story)
Ananci Oyeee!!!
Mamma!!
(Ananci attaches himself to the shadows, he wears a suit with spider's legs painted at the front. His face carries the web of his thoughts. His eyes, the scheme of the Crossroads. He is tying rope for a large web)

Ananci - Closer children, Ananci have a story.a story of a man called Lear

Chorus -   Crick! Crack!

Ananci -
Malick,
an island just off the Coast of Sosconosco
was ruled by King Henry,
Lear's best friend
In Malick, men grew horns according to their behavior,
The worst behaved had the largest horns, while the best
behaved were properly horned.
Women's horns remained unseen, located in a most private
place. They could commit murder and still maintain a
spotless forehead.

7

Kings had absolute power, and consequently very little
conscience.
In Malick, a law had long been passed that Royalty, like
breadfruit trees must hang fruit that carry no seed.
Kings of Malick were forbidden to have offspring,
and so the sound of children's voices was absent from
Henry's Castle.
There was no heir apparent.
When a king did die, the person who became the next king,
was the one most willing to eat the rotting carcus of the last,
with salt,
he had to suck the dead King's bones free of its juices
and belch, loudly in celebration of the having devoured the
stinking flesh.
Such was the politics of MALICK which had become
overwhelmed with men who grew large horns but had
painfully broken them off to hide their ill intentions.
To become king one had to partake of the filth,
place one's mouth securely upon Malick's anus and suck
hard.
The eating of the last King's festering corpse was by no
means a test but the beginning of a long squalid journey,
Would be Kings practised slurping on dead men's intestines
like children feasting on the season's first mango.

From my place on the castle wall I studied the politics
and for what it's worth i'll share my observations with you.

One Cold November
King Henry fell very ill,
Lear, his consort was charged with supervising his treatment

the story began quite simply
Lear was at Henry's bedside constantly,
and I, on his wall listening attentively

(Lear is closer to audience, the bed is in the distance)

Lear - Why don't you just die. **(He looks out the window)**
You've lived a long time..   loved women, laughed with
fools, played the fool.

     I remember that day we saw Hamlet, you laughed at
the grave-robbers until you   cried,   and cried till you
laughed when poor Ophelia drowned, laughing not at the
     mad wet flower but at yourself for crying.
     You held me close that day, chest to chest and
shouted to the court
     " If I should die today! I would   want no one else
     but Lear to devour my   flesh.   Lear shall be the
     next King!" **(he touches Henri's face)** my loving
     brother..
     leave in peace.
(Enter servant)

Servant - how is my Lord doing?

Lear - fine.

Servant - your eyes swell with tears..

Lear - **(aside)**my eyes are fickle

Servant - I'll pray for you both

Lear - **(aside)** pray for us both?

     (The servant kneels in quiet prayer, Lear watches)

     (aside) Shit! **(He looks upward)** I hope his words
     miss heaven. Let the devil abort   these prayers
     lest God hear them and perform a miracle, deliver 20

more years of life to Henry. Even the scent of the thought makes my blood turn white, Unfulfilled ambition is an itch deep inside the ass, bothersome, uncomfortable and inaccessible to solacing fingernails. I can't take this.
(To servant) Boy!

Servant - (stops praying) yes sir?

Lear - get your master a glass of water.

Servant - (pause) yes sir. **(Exit)**

Lear - (kneels to pray) I pray he trips and dies while getting the water. Heaven knows I'll eat his rotting body along with Henri's. **(He looks to Heaven)** Lord! why doesn't Henri die..**(he salivates)**King..Lear. There's justice. All those times I watched you   flaunt your riches. I stood like a dog at a pauper's table, **(Re-enter servant)**

Servant - My Lord.

Lear - What is it?

Servant - the water.

Lear - Leave it there and leave me be.

Servant - Yes my lord **(exit).**

Henry - Water.

Lear - (aside)what's this? a dark miracle?!

Henry - Who is it? I can't see.

Lear - **(aside)**his breath gathers, he may recuperate yet. **(He takes his hand)**

      oh no,no, no. Where's the devil when you need him?

Henry - Lear? Is that you? I feel so much better..**(Lear bites off a finger and spits it out)**   ARRRRH!

Lear - oh God!! **(Lear bites the other fingers clean off)**

Henry - OHHHHHH my hand!!!!
      Will you eat me alive Lear!??!
(pause)

Lear - Hush conscience hush. **(He bites Henri's face)**

Henry - My Face!! Friend Lear..

Lear - I need this. Please forgive me.

(Lear dives for Henry's throat)

Henry -
ARRRRRRRRRRRHHHHHHHHHHHHHHHH!!!!!!!!!!!!!!!!!!!!!!

(Blood is sprayed upon Lear's white clothing)

(Lear stands bloody and alone, chewing the last of Henry, he stares at the audience madly)

Lear - I am king here, for there is none worse here than I

(the servant places the crown upon Lear's head and bows)

11

(the Sailors enter the circle and dance, they strip Lear of his clothes)

Ananci - (center) Time is a Fancy Sailor Mas powdering all who stand in it's path
(The sailors powder Lear and age him, they robe him and leave)
(the court dances into the scene. Lear joins the dance but is eventually left alone after the exit of the dancers)
Remember that law about Royalty not being able
to have children
Well King Lear broke that one, three times,
three daughters, three heirs.
Goneriel, Cordelia and Regan
each named after the mother that bore them
each as arrogant as the court itself.
I despise the court, did you notice?
not the scenes, but the seems,
the pretenses, the lies.
here men can lie and tell the truth both at the same time
like telling a beggar that you'll end his hunger and then you
shoot him, dead.
it's gets even worse when the scenes themselves, seem
and in seeming creates a new kind of scene that
ties me to it simply because I, just, love a scene.
You see the very thing that I dislike is what keeps me here.

Cordelia - Fool ! **(Ananci Scambles for his hat and removes the jacket with the spider icon) (he stands next to her but she cannot see him)**

Ananci - oh, got to go **(to audience)** you see, sometimes I, I play the fool

Cordelia - Fool!

Ananci - and sometimes the Fool plays Ananci?

Cordelia - Fool?

Ananci - Yes lady? **(Aside)** been happening for so long i've forgotton which, is which.

Cordelia - Fool?

Ananci - yes.

Cordelia - where's my father?

Ananci - big question.

Cordelia - eh?

Ananci - would you like to know where your father is, or do you prefer to know where   he thinks he is?
        if it's the latter, I must tell you Cordelia that you should not go there.

Cordelia - why?

Ananci - because it is an insane place.

Cordelia - Fool.

Ananci - yes.

Cordelia - I want to know where my father is.

Ananci - Honestly?

Cordelia - sincerely.

Ananci - Lear is where lear is and no amount of thinking can change that.

Cordelia - where?

Ananci - why in his own head.

Cordelia - and where is Lear's head?

Ananci - you really are the best of the bunch. Governor plum, King Lear's head is in the   chapel and the Chapel is in King Lear's head. Its the first time in a while that both he and his head are in the same place..at the same time **(exit)**

(Cordelia goes to the Chapel to find Lear)

Cordelia - Father! **(No responce from Lear)** Gentle Father..**(still no response)** so warm,   his thoughts melt the bones of his face. why does insanity cling to you sir? **(He flinches and awakens)** Father.

Lear -   Arrrrrrhhhhhh!!! my finger?! They took my finger child. **(He seizes Cordelia and whispers)** I saw them. Last night they took my left toe,**(he shows Cordelia a bandaged toe)** can't let, can't, let..shuu..hush.   **(Exit)**

Cordelia - why can't Father find peace in this warm place, the torment shoots up from him like weeds in a weed garden.
The sea of his face was most calm during the course of my youth,

now it seems that the dark below is bubbling
  upward.
What sins has my loving father not confessed?
Malick is such a peaceful kingdom, but I've heard
  tales from the fool that suggests a bloodier time, a
  time when politics was war and men were actors
  in a savage play of death.
What role did daddy play? Where's the fool?
Fool!

(Enter Ananci)

Ananci - (he hides) damnmit!!

Cordelia - Fool!
(Re-enter Fool)
Ananci - yes M'lady?

Cordelia - know you of My father's past?

Ananci - he,he just did.

Cordellia - what?

Ananci - pass.

Cordelia - fool I said past, not pass

Ananci - oh but the relationship is there and dare I
say,sound.

    For as men pass, they accumulate a past in passing,
    the luggage of that past everyman bears until they
themselves pass.

    where that luggage rests after the owner's
passing..is past me.

    Who's luggage are you requesting?

15

Cordelia - My father's

Ananci - Lear's luggage? Heavy, Heavy burdensome load.

Cordelia - was it painful?

Ananci - oh yes. Yes indeed and not for every back.

Cordelia - please tell me.

Ananci - I shouldn't.

Cordelia - why not Fool?

Ananci - the Burden would become yours and i'm afraid your back seems inadequate.

Cordelia - but father.. lives.

Ananci - where? Certainly not ..**(he points to his head)** here! He's as gone as a mustache in a barbershop.

Cordelia - I must know.

Ananci - Very well Princess.   30 dread years ago Lear..

(He leans and whispers) (the dance tells the story) (he leans away)

Cordelia - oh my God.

(He leans to her again)

oh my.

(She chokes upon her earlier smile)

oh..

**(she slumps to the floor and sits) (Ananci disappears into
the shadows)**

> when grave news comes, she carries a long knife
> that finds new places in the human form to wound.

> now there is a space in my soul that daddy once
filled

> LEAR Ate his best friend alive to become
king..what trepidation.
> I am Princess and heir to horrors.

> What could I say to such a man?
> I've unmasked the devil and found that he is my
father.

> Some inherit peace, others fall heir to violence
> From this day forth, all that King Lear shall hear
from me.. is silence.

(End of scene)
**(The fancy sailors snake through the space in a ghostly
dance, spraying powder into the air as they drift the scene
across to the future)**

**(Enter Gloucester drunk amid the white dust. Edmund
hides in the shadows)**

Gloucester - so much dust, so hard to see things clearly.
> Edgar! Son!
> Always reading, always in the throat of books,
> No one knows his heart's desire.

Like father, like son.

(Pause) I hope not, I read the book Oedipus and got the idea to kill my   own father.

Hell! Those were Cruel times.

Cruel times or Cruel man?
Which is it?

Perhaps it was the dread combination of Times and man.

NO.

It was the book.

Blame the book for influencing a young impressionable mind!

Here's spit for any dog who blames me.**(he spits)**

Ban Oedipus!

I wonder what my own son is reading..

(Enter Edmund)

Edmund - Father.

Gloucester - Edmund, I was just thinking about your brother. Have you see him?

Edmund - No.

Gloucester - you look taller.

Edmund - you're drunk..again.

Gloucester - no!

Edmund - (spits)

Gloucester - (he slaps him)illlegitimate bastard!
Have I mentioned that my loving wife left me upon learning of your   mother's pregnancy, with you?!

Edmund - (aside)Yes you have drunkard, many times

Gloucester - did I tell you that the blasted woman threw salt into the wound by dumping you at my door - step with a note that read " illegitimate relations bring   legitimate guilt in swaddling garments?" I despised her,

Edmund - you hunted her down and had her killed.

Gloucester -(he takes a drink) I was so wrong, acid sins eating me inside out, **(he holds   Edmund close)**
Coke or Pepsi transgressions. They're all the same,
i'm sorry son. So sorry (**he sits and weeps)**

Edmund - (aside) sorry? So easy? My heart is no prostitute's bed that you could tear it   apart and pay me with "sorrys." I will make you pay.
I heard you earlier , you never could keep your mouth shut.
you killed your father to become Earl..
now you suspect Edgar to be capable of doing the same.
(To Father) I saw Edgar today. He was reading.

Gloucester - what was he reading?

Edmund - Oedipus.

Gloucester - Oh sweet lord!

Edmund - Damned Oedipus killed his own father, chopped his head off. They should   ban it. Edgar enjoyed the book though.

Gloucester - he did?

Edmund - never saw him happier.

Gloucester - Oh God!

Edmund - What's wrong Father?

Gloucester - you must listen.
                Your brother wants to kill me.

Edmund -   the legitimate Edgar?

Gloucester - Yes, My son, your brother.

Edmund -   Never.

Gloucester - Yes

Edmund - How do you know?

Gloucester - I just **(pause)** know.

Edmund - He's a dead man. Officer!!

Gloucester - No! We will banish him.

Edmund - he has to die. Banish him and like Oedipus he will return to sever your head.   He must die.

Gloucester - I can't.

Edmund - you must!

(Enter Soldier)

Soldier - Sir. You called?

Gloucester - Sargeant, Find Edgar and..and

Edmund - kill him.
(Exit Gloucester,drunk and weeping)
>   This bastard thing.
>   Its like the wind, you never know its there until it
> affects you.
>   A foul, base, wind
>   with base, with baseness, bastardy base base wind.
>
>   I will master the wind
>   I will be the legitimate, illegitimate

(More wind)
(Enter King Lear with finger bandaged. Regan & Goneril are already seated)
(a jabmulassie-devil dances the dance of the mad)

Lear - I saw a child today, a young child.
>   He'd tied yards of string to a butterfly's tail
>   the butterfly didn't know, couldn't know that he was
> trapped.
>   It Struggled with the wind toward home.

21

And when the butterfly was almost there, the child
tugged the rope backward
     then smiled, like God.

Regan - Father!

Lear - **(aside)**so afraid, like Ravens they wait on my throne
..i need to..to give them a   share before they devour me.
Ants **(he dusts ants away)** Away flesheaters!
     No, i'll give them a small corner to govern, dull their
ambition,
     Lord! It might just whet their carnivorous appetite.

(enter Cordelia and the fool)

Cordelia - what does father want?

Regan - he never gets to the point.

Goneril - let him finish. **(Aside to Regan)**
     The Fool said he's about to split the kingdom into
three parts.

Regan - one for each of us?

Goneril - the way things are going, he just might give it all to
the fool.

Lear - Goneril.

Goneril - Yes father?

Lear - do you Love me?

Goneril - yes father.

Lear - why?

Goneril - you are the Sun, without you there would be darkness.
    I live for your light.

Lear - Then have some sun**(he takes out a Map of the Kingdom)** one-eight of Malick   shall be yours.

Goneril - one-eight?!

Regan - sit! down!

Goneril - it's not fair!

Regan - Shut up!

Goneril - **(aside)** crazy son of a bitch.

Regan - It's my turn. Father?

Lear - Regan why do you love me?

Regan -   you are my every reason father. Meaning made flesh.

Lear - **(he holds her close)** Dear, Dear Regan. One-quater of Malick is yours today.

Goneril - One Quarter! Father!

Lear - Enough. **(The room falls quiet)** a good chef uncovers his pot but once or twice   while cooking. Keep your lid on child.

Goneril - (aside) Good chef? We'd be lucky if you don't burn the entire kitchen flat.

Lear - Cordelia.

Goneril - (to Regan) the rest is hers i'm sure.

Regan - her's and the fool's

Lear - Fairest Cordelia, what do you say?

Cordelia - nothing.

Lear - Nothing?

Cordelia - Nothing.

Lear - Nothing?!
Then, Nothing will come of nothing **(He grabs her by the arm)** out! Out! Stinking Suzie, pretty pretty, upsetting smell!!

Goneril - he's going mad.

Regan - going mad, he was mad.
He's either sane now or much worse.

Goneril - Father!

Regan - Father! Fool! Do something!

Ananci - I cannot stop the wind.

Lear - (one final push) Ooooouuutttt!
(End of scene) (a storm gathers outside)

(Enter Edgar back-bare in the bushes)

Edmund - Edgarrrr!!!

Edgar - this is the season of madness.
      thank God the sargeant warned me
(Edmund and soldiers are on the far end of the stage)
      my own father wants me dead.

      what manner of politics is this?

Edmund - Edgar!!! The Grim Reaper just asked for you! He
      gave me a message to   deliver**!(he checks
      his gun)** and Death writes his messages in simple
      language   with bitter bitter punctuation, six
      bullets, a full stop, after each one.
      (Whispers to soldiers) Find him and kill him!! if
God gets in your way. Kill him   too**!!(exit)**

Edgar - **(kneels)** oh God.

Edmund - **(voice)** Edgar!!!!

**(Two soldiers stand guard high upon the castle wall
oblivious to the scene at Gloucester)**

Guard 1 - you think it would rain? **(Thunder)**

Guard 2 - no.

(Pause)

Guard 1 - you tired?

Guard 2 - no.

(Pause) (Thunder)
(Pause)
(Pause)

Guard 1 - you say something?

Guard 2 - no.

(pause)

Guard 1 - **(he offers some food)** my wife cooked manicou
                (no response) (pause) want   some?

Guard 2 - no.

(pause)

Guard 1 - I heard the princess was exiled. The king threw
                her out with the fool. (Pause)   figures, he's
                been throwing out so many members of his court
                lately, sooner or later his own daughter had to go.
                But to throw out his favorite goodness, man! The
                others are sure to follow.
                Are you listening?
Guard 2 - no.

Guard 1 - its just a matter of time before he throws himself
                out. **(Silence) (thunder)** you   think it
                would rain?

(Edgar finds a muddy pond)

Edmund - Edgar!!
(Thunder) (the storm continues)
(Edgar covers himself in mud and hides upon a tree)

26

Comon man! You're making this harder on yourself.

(Edmund stands before the tree but does not see Edgar)

Why suffer in the storm? Life is pain. Why bother ?

Just let me know where you are and (he shoots the gun toward the audience)   bang!

Shortcut to heaven.

You're a good catholic boy.

Don't you want to meet God?

Where's your faith?

You christians are such hypocrites.

Edgar - (aside) this mud is miraculous

salvation hides in the filth

thank God for storms.

he will not remain here for too long..

i will escape.

For God is both the sewer and the sky.

Edmund - Damn Storm!

Proof that there is no God.

My fight is just.

Certainly I have been wronged by chance to have a been proclaimed a bastard   and disinherited for it.

Is not my blood, blood?

I should have been born an ant, it would have been just as well

I came with nothing and will leave with nothing but dirt

No! I refuse to accept this!

I will have your land Edgar!

27

And God, if you do exist, strike one for
bastards!**(bullet)**
(Exit Edmund)

Edgar - know your place boy. **(He comes out of hiding)**
    This land is mine. It is my divine right.
    Bastard.
    Why can't you be satisfied with what you have?
    Damn slave mentality.
    Just likeYour mother

    this land belonged to my forefathers, God knows they
fought the devil for it.
    who are you to contest my right?
    God is good,
(the thunder continues)
    and good will prevail.
(Darkness, thunder)

(the fool is in the rain with Cordelia)

Ananci - I do hope you're satisfied.

Cordelia - I am.

Ananci - what you like being wet?

Cordelia - nobody forced you to come.

Ananci - I had to.

Cordelia - well it was your fault.

Ananci - my fault?

Cordelia - you had no right to tell me.

Ananci - no right?

Cordelia - I would never have known what my father did.

Ananci - but everyone else knows.

Cordelia - everyone?

Ananci - except you. Your sisters know.

Cordelia - how could they know and I don't?

Ananci - because you never speak to anyone.
Cordelia - I speak to you. You didn't tell me. **(pause)**

Ananci - Cordelia, there is another reason why I came.

Cordelia - another..

Ananci - yes.

Cordelia - well friend, tell me.

Ananci - I want to be free.

Cordelia - free from what?

Ananci - the court.

Cordelia - free from the court? But you live there.

Ananci - I'm a slave Cordelia.

Cordelia - I don't understand.

Ananci - I'm your family's slave.

Cordelia - but you are like family.

Ananci - I despise the situation.

Cordelia - I don't understand. What kept you there then fool? **(pause)**

Ananci -   I want freedom now. **(pause)**

Cordelia - ok, you're free.

Ananci - just like that?

Cordelia - what did you expect?

Ananci - I don't know.

Cordelia - do you feel any different?

Ananci - no I..
(Thunder)
(enter soldiers)
Guard 1 - Princess!

Ananci - your lunatic father has sent them to kill us.

Cordelia - God help us.

Ananci - I need a weapon!

Guard 1 - Princess Cordelia!!

Cordelia - **(falls to her knees)** dear God..let your will be done.

Ananci - a rock, a branch, a leaf, anything!
(Enter guard 1)

Guard 1 - Princess. Its your father. He's mad.

Ananci - the understatement of the millennium. Just kill us. We didn't need to experience your stupidity before death.

Cordelia - Fool!

Ananci - **(he wrings his handkerchief dry)** the next thing you know he'll want to explain to us that its raining..

Cordelia - Fool. **(pause)**

Guard - princess..

Ananci - not you fool!

Cordelia - let him finish.

Guard - They put your father out in the rain.

Ananci - you mean he's not here to kill us? **(He falls to his knees)** Thank God!!

Guard - the water whipped his skin so hard that he bled.

Cordelia - who did this?

Guard - Your sisters, they've put him out and took over Malick.

Cordelia - they hurt daddy?

Ananci - well yes!

Cordelia - Where are they?

Guard - your sisters heard that Lear went to Gloucester to shelter..

Ananci - where are they fool?!

Cordelia - don't be so impatient.

Guard - they are going there to kill him.

Cordelia - to kill daddy?

Guard - I'm afraid so.

Ananci - I'm tired.

(Pause)

Cordelia - how many of you are there?

Guard 1 - 100 strong.

Cordelia - are you prepared to fight for my father?

Guard 1- to the death madam.

Cordelia - then despite my differences with him, we go to replace king Lear to his rightful   place on the throne.

Guard 1 - yes madam.

Cordelia - fool are you coming?

Ananci - I'm afraid, not.

Cordelia - very well.

(Exit Cordelia & Guard)
(the drunken sailors do a dance of mock prepation for war)

Ananci - what a contrary woman.
    You refuse to speak to your father because of the horrible way in which he   became king.
    Now you're more than willing to fight to the death to give him back the   ignominious throne.
    What is more the woman is certain that I would endorse the insanity and join her   to replace a mad king to the throne.
    What the ass is this divine right business and how does one come about it?
    She and the foolish one hundred are now off to fight for a mad toilet cause.
    And I who desire freedom for all people, stand alone. A fool.
    Well Not any more. **(exit)**

(Gloucester stands with letter in hand)

Edmund - what is it?

33

Gloucester - its a letter from Cordelia. Rebellion is brewing.

Edmund - for whom?

Gloucester - Lear, he is the rightful king.

Edmund - he is a mad dog, where is he?

Gloucester - I hid him in the barn. Why ?

Edmund - the sisters are looking for him.

Gloucester - the sisters? Isn't it enough that they threw their own father out into the storm, what do they want now?

(Enter Regan and Goneril)
(the storm continues)

Regan - where is he?

Gloucester - who?

Goneril - don't play the fool Gloucester!

Regan - where is Lear?

Edmund - he's in the barn.

Gloucester - Son! no!
Edmund - there's more.

Goneril - really?

Edmund - Cordelia is plotting to overthrow you.

He has a letter, here!**(he snatches the letter and passes it to the sisters)**

Regan - Let me see.

Gloucester - i'll see to it that she wins!

Regan - No!

Goneril - you!

Regan - won't!!

(They spring on Gloucester and dig out his eyes)

Gloucester - my eyes!!!

Goneril - **(turns to audience and licks the blood from her thumbs)**
in fact, you won't be able to see anything..

Regan - **(with blood filled thumb)** ever again...

Gloucester - oh God! **(He stumbles out)** The Horrible horrible!darkness!

Goneril - **(places her bloody thumb into edmund's mouth)** I guess this makes you the   new Earl of Gloucester. **(Edmund licks the fingers of both Regan and Goneril)**

Regan - I think I'm going to like you.

Goneril - too late, I like him already.

35

Edmund - (aside) by tomorrow I shall have the kingdoms biggest horns.

(The storm dances into the room)
(Lear is in the STORM)

lear - **(thunder) (he shouts to God)**
Stay your hand you unfair & unjust master!!
Stay your wretched lightening and damn your thunder!
You lead me to this! This La Basse of mind where sins are dumped to eventually   stink the head into alienating itself from itself.
I choose to die,to go to Hell than to live within the turmoil of my own mind.
Send me at once to hell Lorddd, let me rest there!
(Lightening) (Thunder)
(enter Edgar covered in Mud)

Edgar - Lear!

Lear - Thank you Lord! I didn't feel a thing.

Edgar - Lear, I have been wronged.

Lear - (touches his face) such pitiful eyes for a demon.

Edgar - Oh dreadful sight to see the just go mad in the rain.
While the sinful galavant in the sunshine left behind by aborted babies.
And while the lambs sleep,

Butchers wake their mothers with knives that know
no shame, no guilt, no   remorse
    only blood,
    the Soul of sanity leaks from the good
    to fuel the ill intentions of the wicked.

Lear - My God, he's drowning me in miseries!

Edgar - (he attempts to embrace Lear) come come old one
here's some solace.

Lear - no no I may have committed some sins, but I cannot
be so bad as to embrace the   devil as a friend.

(Enter Gloucester with blindfold)

Gloucester - what ho! Who's there!

Lear - It's me and the Devil.

Gloucester - Lear!

Lear - yes! It's me.

Edgar - oh God!
Gloucester - Who is that?

Lear - I said it's the Devil..

Edgar - oh lord..oh Lord..oh Lord

Lear - ...blaspheming ....again.

Gloucester - Your daughters, they blinded me..dug out my
eye,we must go!

Lear - go where?

Gloucester - further South, we must escape them.

Lear - Further South than Hell? My, that must be the bottom of the bottom.

Edgar - (aside) oh grey, grave reality
           to see my father blind.
           He was blind before, as blind as a metaphor,
           a blind metaphor
           the predator metaphor has caught up with
father.
           Cruel, Cruel metaphor

Lear - Miseries! Miseries!
           The devil is a poet!! Ohhhh Belzebub has possessed
           the very words themselves   and plated beauty...with
           the soiled real.

Gloucester - We must depart! To the La Basse cliffs!

Lear - SO there's a La Basse in Hell, no surprise.

Gloucester - Let's Go!

(EXIT ALL)
(darkness)
(A television set suddenly produces the only light in the room)

Announcer - Earlier today, at least 10 hours after the initial explosion
           Members of Parliment were seen on the
           grounds of the Queens Park
           Savannah. Eye witnesses report that the

Parlimentarians drift back and forth from reality like ghosts enacting some sort of live play what is significant though is that neither of them respond to any contact whatsoever from anyone who has attempted this.

Professor - The key to any possibility of explanation for this Phenomenon lies with the   fact that no members of parliment seem to be able to recognize or   acknowledge any components of our reality.

Announcer - so you're saying that..

Professor - the bomb was so powerful that it blew Parliament into an entirely different reality...its as simple as that.

Announcer - I understand the concept, but why does this look so much like a play?

Professor - isn't that exactly what a play is, an entirely new reality that is derived from the   current one and is therefore reflective of that reality even in the ideological and philosophical challenges that the 'play' world presents for the parent reality.

Announcer - I don't understand.

Professor - you should go to the theatre more often.

Announcer - I don't understand.

Professor - Ananci seems to have woven our Parliament into a play, a theatre of reality   altering proportions.

Announcer - Professor is it just me? Or have you realised that the Ananci that we are witnessing here is not quite the same as the mythical Ananci that we are accustomed to. Could you provide any insight regarding why this may be so?

Professor - Well not really, except to say that in his own words, the Ananci character here has refused to play the fool, or to be regarded as the fool for that matter. Frankly, the usual web of trickery associated with the Mythical Ananci is totally absent here. Ananci is not yet in control of his destiny and he recognizes that. **(He ponders)** Ananci just isn't in control. What could this mean?

Announcer - Should it mean anything at all? Maybe its all just a whole lot of nonesense to be disregarded. Maybe. This is sylvia Gall from TTT news saying, goodnight.. and God bless.
(The television switches off)

(Intermission)

(two Guards stand wearily in the forest)

Guard 1 - you ready for this?

Guard 2 - no.

Guard 1 - you want to fight?

Guard 2 - no.

Guard 1 - me neither, **(pause)** I feel as forced**(Pause)** To think I'm going to die trying to replace a madman to the throne. **(pause)**
where are your boots? **(Silence)** where are your boots?

Guard 2 - I gave them to Princess Cordelia...such a sweet spirit.

Guard 1 - naive. **(Silence)** isn't she? **(Silence)** well, isn't she?

Guard 2 - what?

Guard 1 - naive?

Guard 2 - why?

Guard 1 - to fight for a mad cause.

Guard 2 - aren't you fighting for a mad cause? **(Silence)** well, aren't you?

Guard 1 - **(pause)** so you gave your boots to the princess?

(Thunder) you think it would rain?
(Thunder) **(no responce) (Guard 2 dusts his toes)**
(Thunder)

Guard 2 - there's an even bigger question to be answered.

Guard 1 - and what is that?
(Pause) (thunder) (pause)

Guard 2 - why are we here? **(Lights fade)**

41

(darkness) (television)

Announcer - Good evening ladies and gentlemen,
This is a live update from the Capital city of
Port of Spain
I'm afraid the situation here today is very much
the same as before.
Eye witnesses report that Parliamentarians seem
to drift back and forth from   our reality like
ghosts enacting some sort of live play
Experts have already coined a name for the
phenomenon which is dubbed   'Lear
Ananci' due to the display's remarkable
resemblance to William
Shakespeare's 'King Lear' and of course the
intervention of the character
Ananci. What is still significant is that neither
of them respond to any contact whatsoever
from anyone who has attempted this.

Professor - There is some speculation that the visual
phenomenon that we are
experiencing may have less to do with the
Parliamentarians themselves, my guess is that in
some inexplicable way this has more to do with
Caribbean people and our own collective
psyche.

Announcer   - Professor, is there any chance that we may
recover the members of   parliament?

Professor - sorry?

Announcer - Do you think the members of Parliament will
ever be in touch with our   reality?

(The television abruptly shuts off)
(more thunder than ever)
(Regan & Goneril stand together with their bloody
dresses) (Regan looks out the window)

Regan - **(smiling)** I hear the storm is a biting one.

Goneril - the storm's not the only thing that's biting..

Regan - you and your damned conscience

Goneril - i'm wondering if we did the right thing.

Regan - you're wondering?

Goneril - yes.

Regan - **(she laughs)** now?!

Goneril - he is our father.

Regan - he's mad.

Goneril - he used to take me for such long walks..
we'd just keep walking..
sometimes I felt as if he wanted us to walk straight
out of the present right into   another future.

Regan - tell me about the time he actually went mad.

Goneril - why?

Regan - its funny.

Goneril - it was horrible.

Regan - tell me.

Goneril - we were at the market.

Regan - get to the point.

Goneril - you are so horrible.

Regan - go on!

Goneril - The butcher..

Regan - go on!

Goneril - will you please let me finish!

Regan - ok.ok. go on **(she chokes on her laughter)**

Goneril - The butcher...

Regan - (she bursts into uncontrolable laughter) oh
gooosh!!!

Goneril` - that's it, I'm done

Regan - no, please tell me.
(Pause)
        Goneril..please

Goneril - ok,alright.

Regan - yess!!!!!

Goneril - you are so impatient.

Regan - comon, tell me.

Goneril - The butcher **(pause)** daddy ordered porkchops..
        the butcher had an accident, chopped off his
fingers, four of them.

Regan - and daddy?

Goneril - he..he ate the digits, all four.

Regan - then?

Goneril - then he bit off the butcher's thumb.

Regan - he bit off the butcher's thumb. **(She breaks into
        hysterical laughter)** ohhh lorrddd!

Goneril - he never went walking again. Children ran from
him. He couldn't stand it. He   loved children.

(Enter Edmund with horns on forehead)

Edmund - (dripping wet) (thunder)
        The storm is much worse
        as if man is finally receiving the spit he deserves.
        I look to the sky and imagine thousands of angels
perched upon clouds
        spitting violently..at mankind.
        ...and woman..kind

Regan - did you?

Edmund - kill Lear? No.

45

Regan - what happened?

Edmund - The storm. My father is missing also. Swallowed by the storm.

Regan - oh my.

Edmund - what is it?

Regan - its the way you said "swallow".
Goneril - what?

Regan - it just turns me on.

Goneril - whore.

Regan - me?! I heard you last evening, ohhh deeper eddy deeper, into my sea.

Goneril - you were listening?

Regan - (to Edmund) so how was your swim? Eddie?**(exit Edmund)**
        Row, row row your boat, gently down the stream
        merrily,merrily merrily merrily

(Goneril slaps Regan)
        I heard you have the dead sea between your legs.
        Me, I threw a tidal wave into his face.

Goneril - into whose face?

Regan - you didn't know?

Goneril - you? And Edmund?

Regan - I had him first and he was delicious.**(exit)**

Goneril - (turns) (aside)
> truely man's nature is constant,
> as constant as the sweat on a priest's forehead
during a nymphomanic's   confession.
> Men are such simple souls, their desires lead them
always
> it is the secret road to their will.
> Decisions are ours to make for them,
> Refusal to do one woman's bidding is the
> willingness to fulfill another skirt's   whim.
> Any good woman knows this.
> Regan took advantage, and she will pay with her
life, I will see to it.
> Upon her death Edmund will come to me, a servant
to my voice .
> **(She touches her-self)**
> For in the presence of sweet, sapodilla Juices, is the
absence of choice.**(exit)**

**(the sailors begin with a slow traditional sailor dance and
advance into a Carib war dance then finally a Sailor
dance)**
(the fool prepares to address the slaves/audience)

Fool -
All of mankind are slaves,
beaten by the whips of time.
We bleed hopes,
perspire dreams and become grey as black life is drained
from our hair.
I have seen men bend to the influence of the time, saw
ambition curl away from adversity to bury Will below
cowardice and its vomit,stillness.

Yet a few men do stand, unmoved, their thoughts charge against the natural flow of the period.
Their voice, it becomes a sail which harvests the reasons of men, the aspirations of nations,
the desires of Gods to eventually change the very nature of the time itself.

you see, the experiences of the many are determined by the will of the great few.
Alas, I am not one of those few, I am naught but a fool and a slave.

A slave to the dreadful Court.
Slave to the mad court, (thunder) mad king, et insane al.
our color restrains us, they say
we are not men, they say
we have no voice, they say
we cannot manage our own destiny, they say.

I say, that my color is a blessing
I say, that I am a man
I say that my voice is God's voice and that my destiny has already began to unfold, in!..my!..own!..hands!

Brothers! Sisters! Slaves!
Let us stand against the tide of time.

Chorus – Against the tide of time
            Against the tide of time **(continue)**

Let us declare that we are free men!

And should we die doing this, let us be remembered by our resistance.
We shall say to the court,

That the Great few are here, We have arrived to change the very nature of Malick.
(stop chorus)
(Looks to the audience)

stand and be counted.
(The audience stands) (darkness)
(Thunder)

Barefoot Soldier - Princess, We are surrounded...Princess

Other soldier - I fear death.

Cordelia - then leave.

Other soldier - I..

Cordelia - Leave!

(Exit Other)

Cordelia - Gather the men.**(to Barefoot soldier)**

Barefoot soldier - princess, they are all dead.

Cordelia - then gather their ghosts.

Barefoot soldier - i think the fool was right to leave.

Cordelia - what? where's my sword?

Barefoot soldier - we've lost it. We've lost, everything.

Cordelia - we should not have come.

Barefoot soldier - did my 100 men die in a play? Is this
not real? or is this some
Malick Macbeth? Had you stepped on
an ant you would have mourned
longer.
(aside)
Such callous insanity and yet she does
not seem mad.

My God, Do the rich think that we exist
only to fulfill their
obsessions?

(A trumpet sounds in the storm)
(Barefoot soldier turns)
(the sailors begin with a slow traditional dance)

Barefoot soldier - Princess, i'd like to have my boots back.

Cordelia - what?

Barefoot soldier - i'd like to have my boots back.

(Enter Edmund and sisters)
(Edmund grabs Cordelia by the neck, his horn scrapes
her arm)
(Regan gives him the noose)

Edmund - It will fit her pretty neck

Goneril - (grabs the rope and roughly places it onto
Cordelia's neck)
so her neck is pretty
(she adjusts the rope)
well her neck is going to be much smaller.

Regan - look, she's jealous **(she laughs) (to Edmund)** kill the soldier.

Cordelia - No!

Regan - what! She speaks?
　　　　(To soldier she hands Edmund a Bois)
　　　　what about you, you have anything to say before you die?

Soldier - nothing.

Goneril - nothing?

Soldier - nothing.

Edmund - then nothing, will come, of nothing.

(thunder)
(The sisters freeze)
(he raises the stick Edmund and the soldier fight in a traditional Stick-fight dance the soldier dies)

Cordelia - I am truly sorry.

Soldier - such pretty vanity, Princess..I was fighting for my own life, and not for your　　　　datoor war **(he dies)**

Edmund -
　　　　how could one man have so much blood?
　　　　Did his blood stain you?
(He touches Cordelia's face,)
　　　　there's some on you.

Goneril - so much blood.

Edmund - Politics is bloody.

Goneril - It would appear so
        the history of this place demands blood, demands souls.

Regan - Shut your mouths!
        you all sound like veternarians who became butchers due to hard times
        Curse your damn prayers and poetics before, during and after the slaughter...
        Just kill the damn animal and move on!

Edmund - a woman after my own heart **(he embraces Regan and kisses her)**

Goneril - **(aside)** soon she will have no heart .

(they depart dragging Cordelia by the neck with the noose)
(enter Lear in the rain)

Lear - I'm alive. The poet certainly was not the devil,
        just another bad poet.

Edgar's voice - Learrr!!!!!!

Lear - it was the mosquito, it was.
        With bite so superficial that one had to question the validity of this..hell
        Mosquitos in hell, the devil himself would drink my blood.
        Such was the nature of my crimes

Gloucester's voice - Learrrr!!

52

Lear - arrrhh! The bacchanal in Malick is the war of my head.

My shame, my daughters, my wretched society at its very worst.

yet it is not so bad, Cordelia is good, she is my hope. A good soul, she shall make   great Queen.

Edgar - Lear!

Lear - to Malick **(exit)**
(enter Edgar & Gloucester)

Edgar - he is not here.

Gloucester - Madness has the devils permission to go anywhere it pleases.

We won't find Lear.
Where are we demon?

Edgar - I am not a demon, I am..

Gloucester - it does not matter.
Where are we?

Edgar - the La Basse cliffs

Gloucester - take me to the edge and leave me.
Let the abyss consume me and my sins.

Edgar -   you mean suicide?

Gloucester - I mean death.

Edgar - you seek escape.

Gloucester - I   require salvation.

Edgar - You crave forgiveness.

Gloucester - and I will not find it on this earth.

Edgar - so you seek to cradle yourself in death?

Gloucester - none else will comfort me.

Edgar - your son will comfort ..and forgive.

Gloucester - my son. A banished flower.
         Cloaked in my sins, I saw him through my cruel
window to be as rotted   as the worst
thoughts of myself.
         It was not so

Edgar - what if your son could forgive? **(He wipes his face
free of mud)**

Gloucester - devil you torture me.
         Just let me die, escape to hell, or is this hell?

Edgar - this is heaven, here's your son.**(he takes
         Gloucester's hand and traces his   face)**
         and he forgives you.

Gloucester - Son.

Edgar - Father.

Gloucester - Thank you devil.

Edgar - the devil is gone father. Gone forever from our lives **(he lifts Gloucester)**

Gloucester - isn't it ironic that darkness could lead me to you.

Edgar - the greater irony is the truth that the light hides.

(Enter Soldier 1 desperately trying to catch his breath)

Soldier - I saw them!!!

Gloucester - Son, what does the light bring now.

Edgar - a soldier.

Soldier - no more!

Gloucester - a deserter, whose army.

Soldier 1 - The mad Cordelia.

Gloucester - Kill him.

Soldier 1 - my God, insanity is everywhere

Edgar - How is Cordelia?

Soldier - as insane as Malick itself
          She led us into an ambush, ignored our warnings
          and knelt in prayer as they slaughtered my comrades.

Edgar - who ambushed her?

Soldier - why, your brother. His horns, huge, like a satyrs long purple.

Gloucester - ohhh!

Edgar - is Cordelia alive?

Soldier - from the bushes I saw them drag her by the neck.
        Sweet soul, she resisted the long noose that held death at arms lenght
        watched her sisters as they spat on her.
        Edmund will kill her.

Edgar - then Edmund must die.

Gloucester - he is my failure.

Edgar - he has failed himself. **(He cleans his stick to prepare for battle)**

Gloucester - he is your brother.

Edgar - **(turns to leave)** he is already dead.

Gloucester - you can't!

Edgar - I will.

Gloucester - noo!

Edgar - **(He moves to exit) (pause)** Soldier, take care of my father.

Soldier - **(pause)**your father, is dead.

Edgar - I will remain here then.
       For as God is my witness in this torturous reign
       brother will not kill brother, Gloucester did not die in
vain.

(Darkness) (the dead soldier enters, powdered, and dances the traditional sailor dance) (exit soldier)

(Lear is being held by Edmund)

(a drum beats constantly)

Lear - unhand me! **(Regan signals to Edmund to free him with a shake of the head)**
       where is Cordelia!?

Regan - in the dungeon!

Edmund - where she will die.

Lear - **(runs toward edmund)** you first!

(Edmund knocks him down with a flick of the wrist using his Bois/stick)

Lear - **(reaches pitifully from the ground)** Goneril.

Goneril - **(she embraces him)** father, I am sorry.

Regan - separate them, she's making me sick **(she holds her stomach)**

Edmund - what's wrong?

(Regan bends over in pain)

Goneril - she is poisoned.

Edmund - poisoned?

Regan - the bush tea, it was..

Goneril - poison.

Edmund - Poison in the tea! **(Regan dies)**

Lear - (Lear storms off stage) Arrrrrrrrhhhhhhhhhh!!!!

(Goneril and Edmund face each other. The sailors enter and dance between them..waiting)

(she reaches to embrace him) (he pushes her away)

Edmund - away woman!

Goneril - I love you.

Edmund - Damn wasted! Wasted efforts!!!

Goneril - what are you saying?

Edmund - I am already dead, woman. I drank one half of Regan's tea.

Goneril - one..time..too..many.

(Goneril turns to walk slowly out, enter Lear with the dead Cordelia, Edmund drops to his knees)
(the sailors dance slowly in the background)

Lear - there. Can't you see them?

58

There! Fancy Sailors dancing in the spaces between the spaces.

Here, and not here.

Waiting, dancing in, time. **(Pause)** the butchers killed Cordelia!

Stifled her with her own scream, did you not hear it?
(Enter Ananci)

Goneril - its the fool.

Fool - Out side gathered are 1.5 million men, women and children,
slaves all.
we are prepared to fight for the freedom that is rightfully ours,
we are all willing to die for control of Malick.

(edmund buckles over, dead)

Goneril - take it, take it all. Its yours.

(Goneril takes her father by the shoulder and slowly leaves)

Lear - fool, I have a joke, a cruel joke.
A bitter joke, acerbic,biting, messy history,
painful days,
the joke is no longer funny.
and the joke is on meeee...**(he cries bitterly)**

(Lear becomes a butterfly and dances between the sailors)

Fool - what is he doing?

Goneril - he thinks he's a butterfly.

Fool - how would the people understand this?

Goneril - they will understand.
(She turns to Lear) Father.

(She walks slowly offstage, following Lear the butterfly, and the dancing sailors)

(There is a loud uproar, thunder, then utter silence)
(Re-enter Goneril to a saddening single drummer)

Goneril - It's Father, the crowds, the people,
   They ate him...alive.

(She cries uncontrolably)
(the stage is silent, all becomes dark except for one spotlight on the fool who slowly dresses himself with the Jacket with the spider's legs)

(Ananci turns to audience)

Ananci/fool - crick, crack

(darkness)

Announcer - Good evening again ladies and gentlemen,
      This is a live update from the Capital city of
Port of Spain
      I'm afraid the situation here today is very much
the same as before.
      Eye witnesses report that Politicians seem to
drift back and forth from   our reality like
ghosts enacting some sort of live play
      Experts have already coined a name for the
phenomenon which is dubbed   'Lear

60

Ananci' due to the display's remarkable resemblance to William   Shakespeare's 'King Lear' and of course the intervention of the character Ananci.

what is still significant is that neither of them respond to any contact   whatsoever from anyone who has attempted this

Professor - There is some speculation that the visual phenomenon which we   have been experiencing may have less to do with the Politicians themselves, but in some inexplicable way this has more to do with Caribbean people and our own collective psyche.

Announcer   - Professor, is there any chance that we may recover the members of   parliament?

Professor - I..

Announcer - Professor, do you think that the members of Parliament will ever be in   touch with our reality?

(She waits, but he does not respond)
(The television shuts off)
(more thunder than ever)

The End.

All praises to Jehovah God in whom all things are made possible.

Made in the USA
Middletown, DE
28 December 2021

57203211R00035